The Heavy Hippo

T0042289

Ruth Wong
Illustrated by Chantal Stewart

We went to the science museum.
My friend Annie came, too.
We had fun in the animal section.

Science Museum

We saw a picture of a baby giraffe.

"Look, Dad!" I said. "You are as tall as that giraffe."

"We are both six feet tall, and it's only a baby!" laughed Dad.

17
16
15
14
13
12
11
10
9
8
7
6
5
4
3
2
1
feet

We saw a picture of a condor.

"Wow! Look at how wide
its wings are!" said Annie.

"They are wider than my arms,"
I said.

3
4
9
10
feet

We saw a picture of a kangaroo.

"A kangaroo can jump 25 feet!" said Mom.

"That's a long way!" said Annie.
"I can only jump three feet."

3
9
8
3
2
1
feet

We saw a picture of a cheetah.

"Can I run as fast as a cheetah?" I asked.

"No," laughed Dad. "A cheetah can run
70 miles an hour!"

"Everything is faster, taller, or bigger than we are,"
I said.

Cheetahs can run up to 70 miles an hour.
Your speed 4 mph

We saw a picture of a hippopotamus.
"The hippo weighs more than both of us!" I said.

"Let's see if all of us would be as heavy as a hippo," said Mom.

"The hippo still weighs more than all of us!"
we laughed.

Some other people were watching us.

"We'll help," they said.

Your weight in pounds
0
4000

They all got on the scales with us.

"Now we are as heavy as a hippo!"
I said.